MW01051266

WITHDRAWN FROM
HERRICK DISTRICT LIBRARY

Succulents

June Loves

HERRICK DISTRICT LIBRARY
300 S. River Avenue
Holland, MI 49423

APR 1 3 2005

CHELSEA CLUBHOUSE

An Imprint of Chelsea House Publishers
A Haights Cross Communications Company

Philadelphia

This edition first published in 2005 in the United States of America by Chelsea House
Publishers, a subsidiary of Haights Cross Communications.

All rights reserved. No part of this publication may be reproduced or transmitted in any
form or by any means without the written permission of the publisher.

Chelsea House Publishers
2080 Cabot Boulevard West, Suite 201
Langhorne, PA 19047-1813

The Chelsea House world wide web address is www.chelseahouse.com

First published in 2005 by
MACMILLAN EDUCATION AUSTRALIA PTY LTD
627 Chapel Street, South Yarra, Australia 3141

Visit our website at www.macmillan.com.au

Associated companies and representatives throughout the world.

Copyright © June Loves 2005

Library of Congress Cataloging-in-Publication Data
Loves, June.
    Succulents / June Loves.
    p. cm. – (Plants)
    Includes index.
    ISBN 0-7910-8266-0
    1. Succulent plants – Juvenile literature. I. Title.
    SB438.L68 2005
    635.9'525–dc22

                                                      2004016337

Edited by Anna Fern
Text and cover design by Christine Deering
Page layout by Christine Deering
Photo research by Legend Images
Illustrations by Melissa Webb

Printed in China

Acknowledgements

The author and the publisher are grateful to the following for permission to reproduce
copyright material:

Cover photograph: Barrel cactus blooming, courtesy of John Cancalosi/AUSCAPE.

John Cancalosi/AUSCAPE, pp. 1, 10, 13; Jeff Foott/AUSCAPE, p. 12; Stan Osolinski-
OSF/AUSCAPE, pp. 3, 19; John Shaw/AUSCAPE, p. 18; Australian Picture Library/
Corbis, pp. 17, 28; Australian Picture Library/ Wolfgang Kaehler, p. 27; Brand X
Pictures, p. 14; The DW Stock Picture Library, pp. 5, 6, 21; Getty Images, p. 20; Wade
Hughes/Lochman Transparencies, p. 25; Jiri Lochman/Lochman Transparencies, p. 9;
Len Stewart/Lochman Transparencies, p. 15 (bottom); Photodisc, pp. 4, 7, 16, 24, 26,
30; Photolibrary.com, pp. 11, 15 (top), 29; Steve Lovegrove/Picture Tasmania Photo
Library, p. 8.

While every care has been taken to trace and acknowledge copyright, the publisher
tenders their apologies for any accidental infringement where copyright has proved
untraceable. Where the attempt has been unsuccessful, the publisher welcomes
information that would redress the situation.

Contents

Plants

Plants are living things. They grow all over the world, in hot and cold places.

Some plants can survive in places where there is very little rain.

Succulents

Succulents are plants with colorful leaves and flowers. They can store water in their thick leaves, stems, and **roots**.

This cactus is a kind of succulent.

Where Succulents Grow

Succulent plants can grow in cool, damp **climates**, as well as in hot, dry climates. They do not require a lot of water to grow well.

Succulent plants make an attractive display in a public garden.

Desert Succulents

Many succulent plants grow in the hot, dry **deserts** of North and South America. Succulents can grow in dry areas because they store water in their thick stems and branches.

These organ-pipe cactuses have stems that look like the pipes of an organ.

Kinds of Succulents

There are many different kinds, sizes, and shapes of succulent plants.

This succulent plant is called an elephant's foot.

Pigfaces

Pigfaces are strong, spreading succulent plants with brightly colored flowers. The leaves have a waxy surface which stops the plants from losing too much water.

Pigface plants help to hold the sand in place on sand dunes.

Cactus Plants

Cactus plants have fleshy stems and branches with sharp spines instead of leaves. The spines protect the plant from being eaten by animals.

Barrel cactus flowers bloom on top of a spiny barrel-shaped stem.

Agaves

Agaves are a well-known group of succulents. They have long leathery leaves that grow in a circular clump.

Agaves grow naturally in North and South America.

Parts of Succulents

Many succulents have a thick, waxy outer layer to prevent loss of water. Roots spread underground to search for and absorb water. When it rains, succulents store water in their stems.

stem

branch

hard, sharp spines grow in a pattern

ridges unfold to store water

The saguaro cactus is a giant desert succulent found mainly in North America.

flowers

Succulent plants have flowers. Special dust at the center of the flower, called **pollen**, helps the flower to make **fruit**, which contains seeds.

pollen

petals

sepals protect the flower before it opens

The the flowers of the saguaro cactus.

How Succulents Grow

Many succulent plants grow from seeds. A seed contains a tiny plant and a storage of food to help the plant grow.

A seed remains in the soil until it is time for it to grow. A small plant grows from the seed.

prickly pear fruit

seeds

slices of prickly pear fruit

The fruit contains seeds for more plants.

The plant grows and flowers. This prickly pear blooms for just one night. Some succulents take many years before they are ready to flower.

The flowers grow
e fruit

New Plants from Shoots and Bulbs

Succulent plants grow from seeds, but they can also grow new plants in other ways. Some succulents send out **shoots** which put out roots of their own and become new plants.

Many new plants have grown from one succulent plant to form a carpet of succulents.

Other succulents, such as yucca, can grow new plants from **bulbs**.

Yucca plants
have stiff,
sword-shaped
int. e

Helpful Animals

To make seeds, succulent plants need a special dust from other plants, called pollen. Succulent plants produce flowers containing pollen and sweet **nectar**. Insects, birds, bats, and other animals travel from flower to flower to feed on the nectar.

A bird called a cactus wren visits succulent flowers to feed.

The pollen in the flower sticks to the body of the animal. At the next plant, some of the pollen falls off the animal onto the flower. This is called **pollination**. The flower then grows into a fruit with seeds for next year's plants.

flower

fruit starts to develop here after the flower has been pollinated

Seeds grow inside the fruit.

Growing Succulents

Succulents are fun to grow. They grow well in containers and in the garden. They need a lot of sunshine and very little water.

Choose a sunny spot to grow succulents.

New plants growing from succulent plants can be cut or broken off. These new plants can then be planted in the garden or in pots.

Watch and wait for new succulents to grow.

Grow Succulents from Cuttings

It is easy to grow new plants from **cuttings**.

What you need:
- leaves from a succulent plant
- seed tray
- coarse soil or special cactus mix
- water

What to do:

I **Spread the leaves in the seed tray and leave them for one week in a warm, shaded spot. The ends of the leaves will seal over.**

2 **Fill the tray with soil and plant the leaf cuttings.**

3 Place the tray in a warm, shaded spot and water lightly.

4 The cuttings will sprout roots and soon you will see the buds of new leaves.

Tips for Gardeners

When growing prickly cactuses, you need to handle them carefully.

- If you need to handle a prickly cactus plant, wear gardening gloves to protect your hands and pick up the cactus with strong paper.

A jab from a cactus spine can be painful!

- Check the roots of pot plants when they have grown. If they look tangled, move your plant to a bigger pot.

- Always wash your hands and scrub your nails when you have finished handling soil.

It is time to move this plant to a bigger pot.

Useful Succulents

The fruits, leaves, and flowers of some succulent plants can be eaten. The seeds of many cactuses can be ground to make cakes.

The leaves of the nopalito cactus can be used to make tasty salads.

The leaves of succulents are used in skin creams, shampoo, and other cosmetics. Scientists are researching ways to use succulent plants as medicine.

The aloe vera plant is useful because of its pleasant smell and soothing oil.

Useful Fibers

Fibers from the leaves of many succulents, especially agaves, are used to make a tough material called sisal. Sisal is used to make ropes, mats, and baskets.

The fibers from these agave leaves will be made into sisal.

Animal Homes

Many animals like the shade that succulent plants provide in hot, dry areas. Some woodpeckers make holes inside saguaro cactuses to live in. Years later, other birds, such as cactus owls, use the holes for a nest.

When cactus owls nest in the saguaro cactus they are safe from their enemies.

Amazing Succulents

The tallest cactus is the saguaro cactus. When a saguaro is 10 years old it is still only about 4 inches (10 centimeters) high. A 200-year-old saguaro is about 50 feet (15 meters) high.

Saguaro cactuses grow very slowly. This one could be more than 100 years old.

Glossary

bulb   an underground stem that stores food and water for a plant

climate   the usual weather in a place

cutting   a piece of a plant that can be grown to make a new plant

desert   a very dry place with few plants

fiber   fine threads that are part of the structure of plants

fruit   part of a flowering plant that contains seeds

nectar   sweet liquid made by flowers which attracts animals and insects

pollen   fine yellow dust made in the center of a flower

pollination   movement of pollen from one flower to another

root   part of a plant that grows down into the soil and takes in water and nutrients

shoot   young branch or stem of a plant

Index

WITHDRAWN FROM
HERRICK DISTRICT LIBRARY